WOW

MOMENTS

Fifty Thank-Yous
And Ten Curses

A Customer Service Story

by Jeff Shapiro
President of Python EFK, Inc.

COMING SOON BY THE AUTHOR:

*Egg Rolls And Electric Cars: Three Companies Establish Quality
Cultures Through Basic Quality Tools And Quality Circles*

WOW

MOMENTS

Fifty Thank-Yous
And Ten Curses

A Customer Service Story

by Jeff Shapiro
President of Python EFK, Inc.

ISBN: 978-0-9773006-1-7

Library of Congress Control Number: 2015901961
Python EFK, Inc., San Antonio, TX

Python EFK, Inc. books are available at special quantity discounts to use as premiums, sales promotions, or for use in corporate training programs. For more information, please write to Director of Special Sales, Python EFK, Inc., 14123 Kings Meadow, San Antonio, TX 78231. Or e-mail us at books@pythonefk.com with the subject line "Quantity Discounts."

Dedicated to all those I've thanked in this book and to so many more. There could never be enough pages to thank you all.

Jeff Shapiro is the President of Python EFK, a provider of Six Sigma, lean, and new product development training and support. The firm also provides project management, employee development, and sourcing solutions.

Shapiro has over twenty years of engineering and management experience in the automotive, consumer product, and medical device industries and has coached and consulted with a wide variety of businesses and business owners.

Jeff's domestic experience is augmented by international assignments in Japan and Mexico. He has a BSE in Electrical Engineering from the University of Michigan-Ann Arbor and an MBA from the University of Chicago.

TABLE OF CONTENTS

INTRODUCTION

Do you remember the feeling you would get as a child when your parents would give you a dollar at the mall and let you run off to the game arcade? What about the flashing lights and sounds when you would get there? You could feel the bass from Space Invaders or the latest hot game thumping through your body.

Do you remember going to your first professional baseball game as a kid? As I'm writing, I can smell the food from the concession stands, see the green grass and groomed infield, and hear the crack of the bat.

In both cases, I remember that feeling I would get in the pit of my stomach. Those butterflies or that feeling of excitement isn't something I often feel as an adult, but it's how I picture the feeling I want to give my customers when I provide a wow moment. If I can provide the level of customer service that gives them that feeling, I know they'll keep coming back to do business just as we addictively asked our parents for another dollar to play games or begged for another summer night at the ballpark.

The following story is personal. While Allen and Danielle are fictional characters, the coffee shop exists and everyone mentioned in the thank-yous is someone I have known or met. I can't thank them enough for having impacted my life. The stories told in the curses section are also true and are not meant to embarrass or cause harm to any individual or organization. If you work for one of these institutions, realize that I'm a former or soon to be former customer and do what's under your control to keep me or win me back.

This book is intended to be the first step on a journey to wow your customers. If you would like help along the journey, Python EFK would love to help you. And hopefully we can give you that feeling we had as kids when we were wowed by the game arcade and our first professional baseball game.

Jeff Shapiro
President, Python EFK, Inc.
shapiroj@pythonefk.com

CHAPTER 1

THE COFFEE SHOP

The door of the local coffee shop swings open, and a man in a dark blue suit approaches the counter. As he nears, shouts of "Hey Jeff" attenuate from the kitchen, and the young man behind the counter says "Good to see you Jeff. What can I get you?"

Management consultant Jeff Shapiro enjoys coming to this coffee shop over the chain competition. He's not treated like a number here. In fact, since he often uses this location as a second office, he's well known to the staff and the hominess sometimes makes him feel like Norm on *Cheers*.

"Ray, I'll take the Aztec hot chocolate. Heavy on the Aztec."

Jeff has spent the morning bouncing from meeting to meeting with business owners. The spicy flavor from the cayenne pepper in his drink will perk him up and prepare him for his afternoon.

As his drink is handed to him, Jeff notices Allen sitting near the back of the shop. They wave to each other and Jeff proceeds to sit down with him. The two have known each other since high school and often use each other as sounding boards for new ideas.

"Allen, great to see you." They shake hands and Jeff continues. "How's business?"

"Well," Allen pauses for a moment. "It's OK, but this recession is starting to take its toll. I need to do something to *wow* my customers."

Suddenly, Jeff feels a sharp pain in his head like he's just been hit by a lightning bolt. Popular terms like "leverage," "synergies," and "tipping point" on those business bingo cards seem to have died down over the last year or two. People don't even seem to walk around talking about their business mission to "exceed customer expectations 100% of the time." What has replaced these terms and phrases is, among other expressions, to "wow" customers. It's a term that seems to be used indiscriminately, and it's the reason for Jeff's sudden cranial pressure.

"Allen, what exactly does that mean?" Jeff prods.

"Well, it means I want to… well… err… *wow* them. You're the consultant. What does it mean to you?"

Jeff sits for a moment and thinks. "To be quite honest, Allen, I hear the term all the time, but I guess I haven't really thought about it." He scratches his head, and as if the light bulb kicks on or the heat from the cayenne lights a fire under the mouse running around on the wheel in his head, proceeds with his answer.

"First, it means providing value beyond expectation. For instance, maybe you can get a customer out of a predicament or make him better in some way. I remember when someone broke into my house. I was concerned about identity theft, and I called all of my financial institutions. Bank of America was the only one that didn't try to sell me something. They helped me deal with my immediate need rather than trying to increase their revenue. They're more likely to maintain my current business and get my future business because they got me out of a bad situation."

Allen interrupts. "That's a great story, but how is that providing value beyond expectation? Shouldn't they have done that in the first place?"

"You're right, Allen. Maybe I could have used another example like the story I heard about a pest control company's technician stopping her truck to help a stranded woman and her disabled child when they ran out of gas. She calmed the woman and her child, drove down the street to get gas, and returned not only with the gas but also with drinks and some snacks."

"Wow, when was the last time you saw something like that?"

"Exactly... WOW! To conclude my first point, providing value beyond expectation sometimes means going above and beyond the call of duty, but sometimes in an industry where the customer service bar is set low, it just means exceeding that bar."

Jeff continues, "My second point is more applicable to the Bank of America story – what you did was noticed. I definitely noticed their effort to help me."

Now it was Allen's turn to sit for a moment and scratch his head. "But is that all it takes? Is it just about providing value beyond expectation and getting noticed?"

"No. It takes more. Point number three is that not only is what you did noticed, but it's noticed by those who are willing and able to do business with you or to spread the message. We can call these two groups of people customers and carriers. There are often times in my consulting business when I save a client five or ten thousand dollars in a day or a few hundred thousand dollars over the course of six months. The larger amount is visible throughout the organization, but the smaller amounts may be visible only to my day-to-day contacts and not to the person who ultimately pays the bill. I may need a day-to-day contact who doesn't have control over a budget to be willing and able to spread the message about the work that I do, otherwise it's as if my work is invisible and never happened."

There's silence for a moment as Jeff takes a sip of hot chocolate and then picks up where he left off. "My final point is that in today's day and age, a wow moment should be shareable virally with others."

Allen's eyes open wide. "Virally? You mean you're trying to spread some sort of disease or something?"

"Not quite a disease," Jeff replies. "But you do want your wow moment to be infectious in a way. If it's memorable and really stands out, maybe you can let a wider audience know about it on Facebook, YouTube, or some other form of social media. In a perfect world, your customers will do the work for you and post it themselves."

Allen smiles. "I really do want to wow my customers, but you were right. I hadn't thought about what that meant. I have to get back to work, but maybe we can get together next week to talk about this some more."

As they say goodbye and Allen jumps in his car to drive off, Jeff remains at his seat in the coffee shop. He jots down his four points in his tablet PC, and stares into the distance. Something is bothering him.

WOW MOMENT CRITERIA

1.	Provide value beyond expectation.
2.	What you did was noticed.
3.	Not only was it noticed, but it was noticed by the person or people who are willing and able to be customers or carriers. *Customers* are willing and able to do business with you. *Carriers* are willing and able to spread the message.
4.	Shareable virally with others.

THINGS TO CONSIDER

- Are there other criteria you would use to define a wow moment?

- Are there times when you've had what you would consider a wow moment when not all of the criteria have been met or they've been offset by the product (i.e. criteria #1-3 were met due to tremendous service at a restaurant, but the food wasn't anything special)? Is this really a wow moment?

- Can an organization create a cumulative wow moment by giving a customer a collection of mini-wow moments?

CHAPTER 2

BRAINSTORMING

An uneasy feeling comes over Jeff as he continues to sip his hot chocolate. Although he has repeatedly heard the term "wow" thrown around, he hasn't previously put much thought into it.

What was his most recent wow experience? He can't think of any. He's had good experiences. He's had bad experiences. But he hasn't had a wow experience anytime recently. What bothers him even more is that he can't think of the last time he wowed his own customers.

As he ponders the topic further, he starts to brainstorm from life experiences. He starts to scribble notes about teachers from his youth, religious leaders, and Boy Scout leaders from his path toward Eagle Scout. He considers family members and friends, co-workers and classmates, politicians, and all of the people with whom he has interacted in the non-profit world. He thinks about the professors he had at the University of Michigan for his Electrical Engineering degree and the professors he had at the University of Chicago for his MBA.

He runs off to conduct his afternoon meetings, but his focus keeps coming back to this idea of wowing customers. The last meeting comes to an end, and like a school child waiting for the last period bell to ring, he's off like a shot as he heads home. On the way, he notices that his friend Deborah has posted to her friends on Facebook to watch a television show tonight about funny and sometimes outrageous sayings and curses in different languages. Her grandmother was interviewed for sayings she grew up hearing in Yiddish and her neighbor was interviewed about Spanish sayings.

After dinner, Jeff calls Allen to tell him about his brainstorming session. Allen is impressed and agrees to conduct the same thought process between now and their next meeting.

"Allen, I really struggled at first, but as I thought about these people and what they meant in my life I started realizing that they were the base of my wow moments. Before we get together next week, I'm going to take this exercise a step further. I'm going to write quick, one or two sentence thank-yous to each of them. I'm not going to actually mail them, but I think it will help me really unlock the meaning of wow. Since wow is such a hot topic these days, I may even make a book out of my work and offer to go around helping people wow their customers."

"That sounds like a great idea. Hey, did you see that post from Deborah? Are you going to watch? Do you know Yiddish? You're Jewish aren't you?"

"Yes, I'm Jewish, but I don't know much Yiddish other than some of the words that have made their way into the English language over the years. Hebrew has overtaken Yiddish these days, but my great-grandparents spoke it fluently. It's sort of a mix of Hebrew, Slavic languages, and traces of Romance languages. I'm looking forward to the show. I met Deborah's grandmother once. She says some hilarious things, and just like in other languages, there are lots of outrageous sayings and curses in Yiddish. Don't get me wrong. In the old days, there was a lot of Yiddish theater and one of the well-known Yiddish writers was Shalom Alechem. Today though, a lot of Yiddish has been forgotten and most of us probably only remember the sayings and curses we heard our grandparents or great-grandparents use."

Allen inquires, "Really, like what?"

"Well, one that I know is "*Ale tseyn zoln bay im aroysfain, not eyner zol im blaybn oyf tsonveytung*" or "*All his teeth should fall out except one to make him suffer.*" Another is "*Khasene hobn zol er mit di malekh hamoves tokhter*" or "*He should marry the daughter of the Angel of Death.*" Just imagine those expressions coming out of the mouth of Deborah's eighty year old grandmother."

Allen starts to laugh. "I definitely have to watch tonight, and you just gave me an idea. Those sound like curses someone felt really passionate about in the moment. We've talked about wow moments which are all positive, but everyone has had a bad experience or something that you might call an anti-wow moment. What if you came up with curses like the Yiddish examples you just gave for these negative customer service moments so people think about what not to do?"

Jeff responds, "Hey, that's a great idea. Maybe the book can be called WOW Moments: Fifty Thank-Yous And Ten Curses. I'll try to do them in a funny way that isn't meant to hurt or offend anyone. If anything, hopefully our businesses and the businesses pointed out in the ten curses can learn and get better."

Allen shows his support for the idea and then Jeff hears a commotion coming over the phone line. Allen's dog is barking, and it sounds like someone is home. "Jeff, I need to run. The wife just pulled into the garage. I have to give her one of those wow moments by showing her that I've finished building the deck in time for this weekend's party."

"Allen, didn't I see you start working on that last summer when I came over?"

"Yeah, you're right. She's not real happy that I took this long. She finally gave me an ultimatum last week – finish the project or leave detailed instructions for her next husband. If you don't see me next week, send out the search party."

"Will do, Allen."

THINGS TO CONSIDER

- Who in your personal and professional life would you thank for wow moments?

- How can documenting these experiences help in the transition to thinking about your daily commercial interactions?

CHAPTER 3

THANK-YOUS

A week passes and Allen and Jeff resume their conversation at the coffee shop. Deborah's grandmother lived up to expectations on the television show only to be matched by some of the Spanish *dichos* of her friend and neighbor Maria. Jeff has a binder with a collection of thank-yous he has written. Allen sits down and curiously asks, "So what did you come up with?"

Since Allen and Jeff grew up together and have stayed in touch over the years, the people in Jeff's thank-yous are well known to Allen. Jeff prefaces his remarks by saying the thank-yous are in no particular order and are not all-inclusive. They're simply top-of-mind thoughts to get him thinking about the wow moments he has experienced in his life.

A few notes from the author:

- As you read the thank-yous and curses, let your mind wander. Think about personal, professional, and commercial experiences in your life.

- More detailed stories about each of the people in the thank-yous can be found at www.pythonefk.com

- Sadly, a few of the people mentioned in the thank-yous passed away during the course of writing this book. They will forever be missed.

- Finally, companies, brands, and products mentioned are the trademarks of their respective owners. Some symbols have been shown but others have been omitted for ease of reading.

GRANDPA AND GRANDMA SHAPIRO

Thank you for being role models to our family, for showing me what love and marriage are really about, for exemplifying an unending level of energy and work ethic, and for teaching me to make friends with everyone and to laugh every day.

GRANDPA AND GRANDMA O'CONNOR

Thank you for teaching me the value of life, the importance of making time for family, and that people who leave for work at 5:30 in the morning deserve as much respect as those who are fortunate enough to be able to show up at 8 or 9 o'clock.

UNCLE GARY

Thank you for influencing the reason I believe what I believe, for instilling in me a love of travel, and for our late-night conversations ranging from religion to politics when I'm in England visiting.

MOM, DAD, AND THE REST OF THE FAMILY

Thank you for always being there, for teaching me right from wrong, and for letting me figure things out for myself.

MR. STIEPER

You were my fifth grade teacher in a school many of your students didn't plan to attend. When declining enrollment resulted in many of us being bussed to Rogers Middle School, you made us feel like part of a team. Thank you for making us all Stieper Stingrays.

MR. RIVERA

You continued Mr. Stieper's team building by making us all Rivera Raiders in sixth grade. You taught us to accept newcomers to our classroom. Perhaps most importantly, thank you for showing us your computer at a time when not many people had one and influencing the direction of many of our careers.

MR. ZOHAR

You had one of the earliest influences on my Jewish education. I still remember some of the songs and games from your class. Thank you for your enthusiasm and for being a role model.

MR. POMEROY

Thank you for being one of the many Scout leaders who had an influence on our Troop. Although you were never my Scoutmaster, your involvement provided a level of tradition and continuity grounded in what Scouting is really all about.

MR. FLETCHER

Thank you for advising the Leadership Corps of our Boy Scout Troop. You provided us all with life experiences that have carried far beyond Scouting.

MR. LAMBERT

Thank you for your attempts to draw the perfect circle, for closing the blinds so "the Russians wouldn't find out" about what we were studying in ninth grade math, and for giving me a break when I needed it.

MRS. KRISTY

Thank you for making our entry into calculus fun. Speaking for the young men in the class, we would have learned even more if we could have concentrated. You were math's Danica McKellar before Danica McKellar was Danica McKellar.

MR. GREAVES

Thank you for making chemistry fun. Even though I only had you in an advisory role rather than as an actual teacher, I'll never forget the flame throwers you would make. They were the fun side of "mad scientist" as opposed to the contact explosive another teacher would spread in the hallway just prior to the bell going off.

MR. MERIDETH

While many of us were initially disappointed when we got "the new guy from Baaawston" instead of Mr. Greaves for chemistry, you engaged us and made the class about more than just chemistry. As you would walk around class watching us take a test, you'd occasionally ask "Shapiro, what are you on drugs?," causing me to go back and correct a foolish mistake. Even though your politics were completely wrong (just kidding), thank you for being about more than just putting a grade in a book – thank you for teaching us to follow a process.

MR. AGOR

Thank you for making us laugh when you would balance a fake sword on your nose in English class and for making some of us want to write a book someday.

MR. FOGARTY

*You and Mr. Pratt were both tough
on the outside but not on the inside.
Thank you for sunrise sessions
and for teaching us discipline,
preparation, and how to get a point
across in our writing. I've met so
many adults who would be much
further along in life if they had taken
your AP American History class.*

MISS LITVINAS

Thank you for your toughness and your two famous quotes. When students were tired, you would tell us "you'll have time to sleep when you are dead," and when we weren't living up to you standards, we might hear "you are not a scholar or a gentleman." I've never read a group of books since your class that have had such an impact on me. I still hear the voices of the characters and at critical times, I still hear your voice.

MR. COLE

You always taught us to think critically. Your AP Physics students were accustomed to excelling at everything we did, so our first taste of "grading on a curve" was a shock, especially when you weren't afraid to have a mean of 40. Thank you for teaching us to think beyond the information that is handed to us and for teaching us to deal with perceived failure. They've been lessons I've carried with me into college and in life.

RABBI SKOPITZ

You were the first rabbi to whom I could relate. Thank you for being there when my family needed you and for your always thoughtful comments and questions.

JUDY WEINSTIEN

Thank you for helping me with my Bar Mitzvah and for teaching me that not everyone in the world has the same freedoms we have in the US.

MAX GROSS, BERNIE ROTH, AND AARON GOLDBERG

The Spanish Inquisition. Pogroms. The Holocaust. There have too often been events in history that have caused Judaism to have to think about survival and continuity. As pillars in our congregation, thank you for passing down traditions to me and teaching me the concept of dor l'dor, from generation to generation.

AARON KRISS

Thank you for your friendship, for easing my concerns as I became a Freshman in high school, for teaching me to make flash powder, and for your brotherhood in NOPAKS.

JERRY ENGEL AND JOE GENIER

As my basketball coaches, you taught me to be a better player and a better young man. Jerry, when I need a burst of energy, I often hear you yelling "Raw meat" and picture Steve Cidoni crashing the boards for a rebound. Joe, when I'm outnumbered and overwhelmed, I think about our short-handed team and your joking reassurance in the huddle that you were "going to let us all play the fourth quarter." It keeps me focused on completing the task at hand.

MIKE BRIGGS

Our Boy Scout Troop often interacted with your Troop from the Rochester School for the Deaf, but it wasn't until summer camp that I saw what a tremendous athlete you were. Later, I would read about some of the colleges that were recruiting you for basketball and their reluctance to sign you since they couldn't figure out how to deal with your deafness. What they didn't see was how your lack of hearing heightened your other senses. Thank you for teaching me that an obstacle to some doesn't determine the whole person and can be offset by other strengths.

KEN MICHAEL

Thanks for giving me my first meaningful job repairing calculators and computers. Although I had previously been employed, my time at DOX Electronics taught me business lessons I still use today in my own business.

MUSTANSIR MIR

Your Introduction to Islam class was fascinating, but the way you taught the class was even more impressive. The class was filled with students with different backgrounds, different faiths, and even different beliefs within these faiths. You asked all of us, Muslim and non-Muslim alike, to put down any of our preconceived notions and learn about the beauty of a religion. Thank you for your balanced and tolerant approach.

NEIL SIMPSON AND ALEX MARSHALL

Thank you for teaching me about perseverance. As roommates and teammates on the football team, it must have been difficult when one of you would get playing time and the other was hurt, but you kept your heads up knowing that the roles could reverse at any time.

LEROY HOARD

Most people run with their feet. You always ran with your heart. Thank you for teaching me to run with both.

DESMOND HOWARD

You're the fastest person I've ever met. Thank you for teaching me that we all have another gear.

LANCE DOTTIN

You always showed character and composure. When someone would scramble for a particular jersey number in Intramural Basketball, you would let him know that the number on the outside didn't matter. It was what was on the inside that counted. Thank you for being about doing, not just talking.

BO SCHEMBECHLER

There aren't many coaches like you today. When I would see you leaving for the day as we prepared for Intramural Football, it was like looking into the face of a deity. Thank you for your discipline and your character. The world could do with a few more Michigan Men.

DR. MARSDEN FOX

Some doctors know how to deal with kids and some don't. You would think this would be a prerequisite for a pediatrician. On behalf of all of your patients over the years, thanks for always putting my mind at ease during my visits.

DON EISENSTEIN

I read <u>The Goal</u> by Eliyahu Goldratt before I ever had any manufacturing experience and again in your class. You took what I had initially read and turned it into a completely different book by adding depth to the study. Thank you for teaching me to read below the surface and for encouraging me to further my Production and Operations Management knowledge.

ROBERT GREEN

You're either the craziest professor I've ever had or the most brilliant, or both. Thank you for not only teaching me to think "outside the box," but also to think big.

ART MIDDLEBROOKS

Thank you for furthering my knowledge of new product development and for the opportunity to lecture in your class at the University of Chicago. Having spoken to a U of C MBA class and been barraged with well thought out questions, I know I can speak to anyone, anywhere.

JAMES SCHRAGER

Your Venture Strategy class inspired me to start my own business. Of course, your teaching method and unrelenting style of questioning prepared me well. Thank you for being more than a professor who "professes" – you're a true teacher.

MORIO TAKAHASHI

Thank you for the opportunity to learn about Japan first-hand during my year assignment as a young engineer at Technical Auto Parts, and thank you for making me feel like part of the family.

JOHN GALAN

We worked together twice. Thank you for introducing me to new product development making Ray-Ban® sunglasses at Bausch and Lomb, and thank you for teaching me about leadership and dealing with difficult situations.

JOHN OAK AND LARRY BRAND

Thank you for your lessons in project management and for emphasizing that everyone in an organization is equally important.

BOB FEY

You weren't the easiest person to work for at Owens-Illinois, but I've carried forward my experiences with you and I thank you for the tools and techniques I find myself using when I'm in a plant management or restructuring role.

BILL SCHMITZ

You were my mentor at Bausch and Lomb. Thank you for showing me how much can be accomplished by surrounding ourselves with a talented team.

MY BAUSCH AND LOMB BROTHERS AND NPD ALUMNI

If you came through Bausch and Lomb's New Product Development (NPD) group in the Eyewear Division, you were part of a special team. We could communicate without talking, we could pick up for each other without missing a beat, and we could be in a van or on a plane on our way to solve a problem at a moment's notice. I'm not sure if I'll ever work with a better group.

RABBI ARYEH SCHEINBERG AND RABBI SAM STAHL

Thank you for your commitment to San Antonio over the years and your tireless effort that has made it the kind of place where I want to raise a family.

MARK FREEDMAN

*Thank you for recognizing that
young people have an important
role in shaping a community
and for your dedication to
bringing people together.*

JULIÁN AND JOAQUIN CASTRO

Thank you for your passion to make San Antonio the best it can be and for being role models to a generation of San Antonians, no matter what their background.

JUDY LACKRITZ, MAXINE COHEN, AND HARRY MAZAL

Thank you for your desire to make the world a better place and the work you each do to make people better human beings.

RACHEL RUSTIN, PETER PRICE, AND DEVORAH COHEN

Thank you for your commitment to education and the styles and energy you each have brought to your work.

MICHAEL BROOKS

We've only had two interactions, but I was tremendously impressed by the fact that you went the extra mile to help answer my questions. Thanks for all that you do at the University of Michigan Hillel and for helping others learn from your work.

SIMCHA STEIN

When katyushas started falling in northern Israel in 2006, you made the tough, symbolic decision as Executive Director of the Ghetto Fighters' Museum to keep the museum open. It meant a great deal to the troops coming back from the front in Lebanon and it meant a great deal to those of us watching with concern from afar.

JIMMY AND DORIS TOUBIN

Several years ago while I was involved with the Community Relations Council (CRC), I was going through an unpleasant time in my life. I put a note in an envelope that said "Do something to be worthy of the Joel A. Toubin Community Relations Award," and the note kept me putting one foot in front of the other on a daily basis. Thank you for your philanthropy, for the unintended positive consequences it has had on me, and for the impact it will continue to have on others.

MICHAEL MURPHY, STEVE SUNDERLIN, MARC ENGEL, TOM BINKOW, AND LUIS SANTOS

We've had deep friendships at different stages of our lives. Thank you for the long conversations, for being sounding boards, and even though I luckily haven't needed it, for being the kind of friends I could call at 2 o'clock in the morning with a problem. I only hope I've been half as good a friend.

CHAPTER 4

ALLEN'S CONSTRUCTIVE CRITICISM

Allen's eyes are starting to spin around in his head as Jeff finishes reciting his fiftieth thank-you.

"That was a great list of thank-yous you put together. It must have taken some real thought. My only question is whether these constitute wow moments."

Jeff listens intently to Allen's feedback and responds. "I was really just trying to get something down on paper, but if I look at the wow criteria, I may agree with you. These all met criteria #1 because these people all exceeded my expectations. They all met criteria #2 because these experiences were noticed. The people I thanked all met criteria #3…"

Allen jumps in. "How can you say they met criteria #3? You never bought anything from most of these people and I'd question whether you made a second purchase from any of the others."

"Actually, Allen, remember that criteria #3 deals with either being a customer or a carrier. In some cases like Don Eisenstein, he had such an influence in my first Production and Operations Management class that I went on to take another class from him. In many of the other cases, I've been a carrier sharing a message about these people. I understand what you're saying though. It's difficult to describe yourself as a customer or a carrier of a family member. I think in a future step, I would use what I learned from these thank-yous to develop thank-yous for truly commercial experiences and transactions. Maybe I can do this when I get to my list of curses."

Allen nods his head in agreement. "There is one more suggestion I would make. While you're a carrier in many of your examples, I don't know if they all meet your intention in criteria #4. These examples may be spreading virally by word of mouth, but they may not be spreading at the viral level you expect from the fourth criteria."

Jeff thinks for a few seconds. "Agreed. Maybe criteria #4 should be a "nice-to-have" criteria."

Jeff and Allen sit back in their chairs. Allen gets a big smile on his face and can't hold back. "Your thank-yous really brought back some memories. What ever happened to Mrs. Kristy?"

THINGS TO CONSIDER

- Is criteria #4 a "must-have" or a "nice-to-have?"

- In chapter 2, you considered people in your personal and professional life who you would thank. Can you think of thank-yous to write to someone regarding commercial experiences and transactions?

CHAPTER 5

CURSES

After some small talk about their high school years, Allen and Jeff get back to business.

"What's next on the agenda?" Allen asks.

"Let's talk about curses," Jeff responds. "I have ten ready to go, and I've been waiting all week to share these with you."

Allen laughs. "It sounds like you're really passionate about your poor customer service experiences. Go ahead, shoot."

Jeff pulls out his list and begins to rant.

CURSE #1

May you live in a cave the rest of your life.

A look of shock covers Allen's face. "Who's that directed at?"

Jeff responds, "Osama Bin Laden!"

Allen is dumbfounded. "What's your problem with Osama Bin Laden other than the obvious?"

"Well, as I see it, he owes me $1,472. First, there is all the stuff I've had confiscated at security checkpoints. Then, there is all the time I've lost taking off my shoes and putting all my stuff in three ounce containers and plastic bags. I know this is sort of a nonsensical one, but I needed to get it off my chest."

To add to author's To Do List: Remember to send thank-you to Seal Team Six.

CURSE #2

May you get an incurable case of bed bugs.

Allen raises one eyebrow and asks, "You're not directing that at me are you?"

"No," Jeff responds. "It's directed at the Hampton Inn®. I had a customer ask me to visit their factories, and they asked me to stay at the Hampton. I set up my reservation through one of the online travel sites and had to book multiple stays at the same hotel location since I was going to bounce back and forth over several days in a three state area. Hampton's online reservation information was like reading a legal document in small type, and I must have missed something that identified one of the stays as non-refundable. Due to an emergency, I needed to change reservations. When I called the toll-free number, it was as if the woman in the call center was reading from a script and wouldn't help me. I called the hotel directly, and a front-desk employee was willing to help, but the general manager was going to have to get involved. After several attempts to connect with the general manager, I ended up eating the cost of the hotel stay. When I rebooked a few weeks later, I chose another hotel and haven't been back to a Hampton ever since."

CURSE #3

May you be forced to drive a Yugo.

Allen chuckles. "This is about that trip we made to Detroit, isn't it?"

"Exactly. Remember our experience at Dollar Rent A Car®? There was one guy working behind the counter, about twenty people waiting in line to get their cars, and three or four employees kept walking in and out of the office without helping the poor guy behind the counter. A few of us were ready to jump in and help the guy if we could have sped up the process."

CURSE #4

May you be water-boarded with hummus.

Jeff lifts up the Star of David around his neck and scratches his chest before placing it back in his shirt. "I fly to Israel once or twice per year. I always enjoy myself until it's time to come home. There are only a few flight options, and I find Continental works the best to get back and forth between Tel Aviv and San Antonio; however, check-in for the return flight is always painful. It seems like a line always closes just as you're getting to the counter, and I had one cancelled flight where after spending what seemed like half the night on the airplane on the tarmac, the staff selectively told people about food and hotel vouchers during the re-booking process. I ended up sleeping on the floor in the airport."

CURSE #5

May you be forced to walk barefoot, live out of three ounce containers, and never be allowed to carry a tool larger than seven inches in length.

Allen listens to Jeff's curse and cuts him off before he can start his explanation. "Jeff, you don't even need to describe this one because I feel the same frustration. There are a lot of good people working in the TSA, but every time I have to pass through an airport, I dread the security line. I never know what set of rules they may follow. At one airport, they may make you take your grooming supplies out of your suitcase, but at the next airport they may not say anything. I had a can of shave cream confiscated that I had taken with me on three previous trips. Apparently, the TSA was concerned that I would shave someone to death in mid-air."

Jeff nods. "Amen, brother. And don't get me started on why we take off our shoes when there are goofballs trying to get on planes with explosive underwear."

CURSE #6

May your phone line be filled with so much static that a lightning bolt shoots through the receiver, into one ear, and out the other.

Allen jumps in again. "You don't have to tell me this one either. I saw your blog post about all of the issues you had with AT&T with your home phone and television systems. How did you ever resolve your situation?"

"Well, Allen. After repeated attempts to maintain a working landline where I could hear someone on the other end, I finally gave up. I work from my office in the house, and it was embarrassing to miss calls from customers or to be unable to hear them through the static when they could get through. I eventually cancelled my landline and referred everyone to my Sprint cell phone. Regarding my television service, I was more than happy to leave my cable company and change to AT&T's U-verse®, but I'm starting to get frustrated with all the times the system locks up. Somehow it always seems to happen when a big play is about to occur in a game or when a mystery is about to be solved in a movie I've been watching for an hour or two."

CURSE #7

May you be stuck in a long-term contract with a faulty technology solution.

Remember when I was looking for a video conferencing solution so I could give my training courses live or on-demand through the internet?" Jeff asks.

"Yeah, I remember. You were very deliberate in choosing a service. It took you almost a year to finally decide."

"Yes, you're right. And I finally chose WebEx® because the demo was great and they appeared to have everything I needed. Unfortunately, they overpromised the integration with credit card processing. When it came time to get things set up, WebEx steered me in multiple wrong directions and the customer support people at the service with which they integrated were very arrogant. Unfortunately, I didn't get the issue rectified before my contract renewed and WebEx stuck me with an extra year of worthless service. By the time I finally could get out of my contract, I was out $7,000 and Cisco® had bought WebEx. I've always been a fan of Cisco, but now they periodically send me an e-mail trying to get my business back. Luckily, I can ignore their e-mails, because I hate to think what direction the conversation would go if I ever spoke to someone on the phone."

CURSE #8

May your children's bank accounts be subject to penalties and interest.

"When I was five or six years old, my parents set up a bank account for me at Lincoln First Bank in Rochester, New York. When it came time for my first interest payment, the bank informed us that my account didn't meet the minimum and I wasn't going to get interest. My parents closed my account and moved it to Dime Bank just a few hundred yards away. I remember the people at Dime being so nice and valuing me even though I was a young kid with a meaningless amount of money in my account. Chase later bought Lincoln First, and to this day I don't do business with them if possible."

"What do you mean?" Allen inquires.

Jeff responds, "My mortgage changed hands since its origination, and eventually ended up with Washington Mutual which was bought out by Chase. It's not like I'm going to go to the effort of moving my mortgage, but I don't go seeking business with Chase even though there is a branch within walking distance from my house."

CURSE #9

May you be treated every day like you treat your customers on your worst day.

"So you don't go looking for business with Chase. What's that bank up north that you've done business with for a long time?" Allen asks.

"M&T, but interestingly enough, I've just ended my relationship with them."

"Why? What happened?"

"They've always been a good bank, and I've stuck with them even though I'm well over a thousand miles away from the nearest branch. However, about a year ago, they mis-categorized a transaction leading to some bank charges. When I finally unwound the issue, I ended up getting mixed up and was hit with additional charges after I somehow stopped getting paper copies of my statements. It turned out I was getting hit month after month with bank charges. When I tried talking to customer service, they acted nonchalantly and didn't seem to want to keep me as a customer so I obliged them. It's too bad, because the branch I dealt with always treated me right. In fact, when I closed my account someone called me to discuss the issue. His call may get me back as a customer someday, but it probably isn't going to happen soon."

CURSE #10

May you be subjected to a month of explosive diarrhea.

Allen grimaces. "I'm guessing this one is about food safety, but I'm not sure if I want to know."

"You're right, and it's about a chain where you've eaten hundreds of times."

"Oh, great. I feel better already."

Jeff proceeds. "I eat at Subway® maybe once every few weeks, but there is a location I can't bring myself to go back to. I was waiting in line when one of the employees filled ice in the drink machine from a dirty bucket. It ranks right up there with seeing a guy step away from a mop bucket to take my order without washing his hands or having someone hand me my food right after taking someone's money. Definite turn-offs.

Allen agrees. "Yeah, when I get a sandwich at Subway, I always ask for Swiss cheese, lettuce, tomatoes, and banana peppers. I generally prefer that they hold the hepatitis."

CHAPTER 6

THEORY BECOMES REALITY

As Jeff wraps up with his list of curses, Allen finishes jotting down some notes.

"If you don't mind," Allen says, "nature is calling. Let's take a break for a few minutes."

Allen heads to the back of the shop and turns the corner out of sight. While he's away, Jeff stands up and takes a moment to stretch and refill his drink. A few minutes later they're both seated back at their table.

Allen starts, "Ready to begin again?"

"Yes," Jeff replies. "What did you write down as I was talking?"

Allen pulls out his list and lets Jeff know that he scribbled down some bullet points based on Jeff's curses or anti-wow moments. "As you were talking, I thought about some lessons we can learn from your examples as well as some things that are relevant to today's economic and technological environment. I'll run through them and then we can discuss them."

- One person, like Osama Bin Laden, can destroy the reputation of an organization or a large group of people.

- Likewise, Subway and Hampton Inn show that a corporate group or a single franchise or location can blow it for an entire company.

- Your AT&T, Continental, and TSA examples show that you can retain an unhappy customer if they have limited options. Unfortunately, they'll complain about you often and leave as soon as they have time to switch to a viable alternative.

- Your Chase and Cisco examples prove that you can lose a customer or potential customer that has nothing against you but has a problem with a subsidiary or firm you've acquired.

- Your Chase story also teaches that a simple, relatively minor issue left unresolved can lose you a customer for a very long time if not forever.

- When you talked about Subway and Hampton Inn, it made me realize that if you allow limited problem-solving authority at front-line levels in your organization, you can limit the ability to wow and may in fact increase the chance for anti-wow moments. Sometimes we put systems in place on purpose to prevent abuse, but employers and employees need the knowledge, trust, and integrity necessary to have systems that allow the flexibility to resolve issues appropriately.

- Along similar lines, you made me think of an experience with a company that uses an overseas call center. I normally have good experiences, but I find that differences in handling issues between the local and overseas centers can be annoying. I find the local teams sometimes have the ability to resolve an issue themselves or have access to someone who is permitted to make a decision. Often when I deal with an overseas call center, it seems like the person is reading from a script and has no latitude or access to a decision-maker.

"Great thoughts, Allen," Jeff replies. "I agree with everything you said and would add one more item about call centers that drives me crazy. When I'm on the phone with someone from India and they start by telling me their name is "Bob," they're already heading away from a wow moment. I realize this is done to make customers in a particular market feel more comfortable, but I'm an adult and have read Tom Friedman's The World Is Flat. If you start off lying about your name, I'm not sure if I trust you during the rest of the transaction and I'm not sure if I trust the company you work for."

"Allen, before you listed your bullet points, you mentioned something about the economy and technology. What were you thinking?"

"Well," Allen remarks, "when the economy was humming along, it seemed like everyone was happy. Don't get me wrong, we occasionally had unhappy customers but we were typically able to resolve the issues. It seems like since the economy turned down, we have more wound up customers needing an outlet to vent. What may have been a minor issue in the past is a major disaster in their eyes today. Unfortunately, technology allows them to blow the issue out of proportion. Once they post a diatribe on the internet, it's there forever."

Jeff doodles on his tablet PC for a moment before looking up and responding. "I've learned a few interesting lessons from these types of experiences. First, wherever possible you should probably try to defuse a situation before it gets to that point. Second, if you're doing a good job and the issue is just an anomaly, you should see ten times as many positive reviews of your product or service on internet sites as negative ones. Third, if this isn't the case, you may have to take a hard look in the mirror and ask whether you really do have an issue that needs to be addressed. Sometimes we want to think of a negative comment as coming from someone who is a crackpot, but we're too close to the process to realize that we do have something that needs to be addressed. Finally, if you are dealing with someone who is out of line with their comments, you have to know when to fight the issue and when to let it die quietly. Sometimes you can throw gasoline on the fire, cause more problems for yourself, and drive more negative web traffic by making a stand."

Allen nods his agreement and asks, "So where do we go from here?"

Jeff thinks for a minute and responds, "Why don't we turn theory into reality. I'll clean up the thoughts we've discussed about wow and anti-wow moments and e-mail them to you. Based on these ideas, we can come up with a gameplan for wowing your customers over the next year."

Jeff looks at his watch and realizes that he and Allen have been so consumed by their conversation that they didn't notice the day was coming to an end. They pack up their computers and briefcases and head out to their cars. They're both about to open their car doors when Jeff shouts to Allen, "Hey, the boss must have found the deck to be acceptable."

Allen smiles. "Yeah, she told me she'll keep me…at least until I finish the next project."

They both share a few laughs and drive off into the sunset.

THINGS TO CONSIDER

- Is there anything else you learned from the curses?

- How have you seen economic conditions, technology, or other considerations impact wow and anti-wow sentiment?

WOW MOMENT CRITERIA

1.	Provide value beyond expectation.
2.	What you did was noticed.
3.	Not only was it noticed, but it was noticed by the person or people who are willing and able to be customers or carriers. *Customers* are willing and able to do business with you. *Carriers* are willing and able to spread the message.
4.	Shareable virally with others.

LESSONS FROM THE CURSES

1.	One person can destroy the reputation of an organization or a large group of people.
2.	A corporate group or a single franchise or location can blow it for an entire company.
3.	You can maintain an unhappy customer if they have limited options. Unfortunately, they'll complain about you often and leave as soon as they have time to switch to a viable alternative.
4.	You can lose a customer or potential customer that has nothing against you but has a problem with a subsidiary or firm you've acquired.
5.	A simple, relatively minor issue left unresolved can lose you a customer for a very long time if not forever.
6.	If you allow limited problem-solving authority at front-line levels in your organization you can limit the ability to wow and may in fact increase the chance for anti-wow moments. Sometimes we put systems in place on purpose to prevent abuse, but employers and employees need the knowledge, trust, and integrity necessary to have systems that allow the flexibility to resolve issues appropriately.
7.	Inconsistency in problem-solving ability/authority and practices that make customers question your integrity can result in unhappy or lost customers.

CHAPTER 7

A YEAR LATER

The man in the navy blue suit sits at his regular table reading the newspaper and waiting for his next appointment to show up. He finishes the business section just in time to see his 11 o'clock standing in front of him with a smile beaming from ear to ear. Allen and Jeff are each a year older and a year wiser. Allen is Jeff's 11 o'clock appointment and today is his day to give a progress report on wowing his customers.

"Allen, let's start from the beginning. What have you accomplished over the past year?"

Allen can't get the smile off his face. "Well, we started by sitting down with the team and having a heart-to-heart conversation about our business and our customers. We talked about the things you and I talked about in our introductory conversations and why it was important to wow our customers. Next, Danielle from your office kicked off our "Year of WOW" by training everyone in our organization. It really helped to make sure we were all on the same page, and we even had everyone sign WOW Contracts stating their commitment to the program."

"During the training, Danielle stepped us through a bunch of exercises. We broke the ice by having everyone come up with someone they would thank in their personal or professional life. This led to an exercise where our team members had to develop a thank-you for a commercial transaction and another exercise where they had to explain what they wanted someone to say about their customer service level. Next, everyone created their own curse and followed up the thought process by explaining what they wouldn't want someone to say about their customer service level."

"Once people got into the flow of what we were doing, we stepped into the next phase. Danielle helped us sit down with each team member and create action plans for the year. It's easy to say we want to wow our customers, but sometimes it requires that we get more knowledgeable about our customers, our products and services, and our processes. By laying out action plans, we were able to identify where people needed help improving, give them opportunities to improve, and follow up regularly throughout the course of the year. Since we wanted "wow" to become part of the norm or part of our corporate culture, we also chose to talk about it in some way at each of our various daily, weekly, and monthly meetings."

"Finally, we learned by doing. Whether we succeeded or failed in a situation, we used it as a learning opportunity to get better."

Jeff cuts in for a moment. "Sorry to interrupt you Allen, but what are some examples of lessons you learned?"

"I'll give you just a few that stand out in my mind," Allen replies. "First, we knew we needed to do a better job capturing wow moments, but we were unprepared. A moment is just what you think it is, a moment. If you don't jump on it immediately, it can disappear forever. We had a few great customer interactions, but by the time we documented them, the moments had passed and we couldn't capture them effectively. Based on these experiences, we decided to get better prepared. Now, we have surveys, testimonial forms, and other templates ready to go in order to immediately capture the experience. Also, when we have an event, we always have a still camera or a video camera ready to go at a moment's notice. We've captured some great customer experiences and testimonials on video because we've become much better prepared."

"Do you have another example?" Jeff asks.

"Yes," Allen continues. "It's related to the first. Since we're so much more prepared, we've documented a lot of customer feedback either ourselves or by knowing how to ask our customers to give us feedback. We've loaded our website with testimonials and video clips, and if you were to perform an internet search about our company you would find that the wow experiences far outshine any negatives. We take all the negatives to heart and determine whether we need to implement countermeasures to make improvements, but we no longer find that we need to fight what we feel are outliers."

Now Jeff has a smile beaming from ear to ear. "So it looks like you've put a good process in place. Tell me about your results."

"First," Allen proceeds, "our relations with our existing customers have improved tremendously. I credit this with picking up several new pieces of business with them accounting for a year-over-year increase in revenue of about 15%. Second, our customers are so happy with us that they tell other people about us. This referral business accounts for 20% of this year's sales. All in all, I can't complain. Business is up, and in fact, I really need to run. I have two interviews to conduct after lunch. We've picked up so much business that we're going through a hiring phase to make sure we have enough capacity to keep up."

Jeff congratulates Allen on all the hard work his company has put into wowing their customers and the results they've had so far. They shake hands, and as Allen departs, Jeff looks off into the distance. If only more companies chose to put in the same hard work to wow their customers…

BRINGING WOW TO YOUR ORGANIZATION

This final section of the book leaves you with some tools and exercises that may be helpful in bringing wow to your organization. There is only so much you can do in a 5.5 x 8.5 inch book. Full-size forms and our ever evolving tools and exercises may be found on our website at www.pythonefk.com.

Good luck with your implementation, and if you ever need assistance, feel free to contact us.

Get ready to kick off your "Year Of WOW!"

EXERCISE #1

Have a heart-to-heart conversation with your team about your business and your customers.

Topics you might cover:

- State of the business.

- What does it mean to wow your customers?

- Why is it important to wow them?

- Who are your biggest customers? Who are your most important?

EXERCISE #2

Collect baseline performance metrics for your business and customer service.

List three ways you measure customer service. Provide definitions and examples of your metrics so everyone easily understands. A table such as the one found on the following page may be helpful.

Use the exercises that follow to get your team thinking about customer service. These can be discussed all at once or periodically throughout your "Year of WOW." Many can be incorporated into your existing training and communication mechanisms with relatively little modification.

Metric	Definition	Example	Frequency To Measure	Who Will Measure And How?	Baseline	Current	Goal

EXERCISE #3

Write three 2-3 sentence thank-yous to people you know personally or professionally. What can these thank-yous tell you about customer service?

EXERCISE #4

Write two thank-yous for commercial transactions you've had. What can these thank-yous tell you about customer service?

EXERCISE #5

Who are your customers and carriers?

How have you wowed one of them?

How could you wow more?

EXERCISE #6

How would you want your customers to describe your customer service level?

How do you get there from your current customer service level?

EXERCISE #7

Write one curse regarding an anti-wow experience you've had.

EXERCISE #8

How have you made a customer want to curse you?

EXERCISE #9

How would you not want your customers to describe your customer service level?

EXERCISE #10

What does your company, organization, department, or process do? Where are the opportunities to wow your internal or external customers?

Remember, it's important to wow your team members and internal customers while you're wowing external customers.

EXERCISE #11

What are five ways you could wow your customers, keeping the four wow moment criteria in mind?

Are you ready to create an action plan to make this happen?

1.

2.

3.

4.

5.

EXERCISE #12

Create an overall (company, organization, department, or process) customer service action plan for the year.

THINGS TO CONSIDER:

- Will you tie wowing the customer to performance evaluations?

- How will you incorporate new team members into your "Year of WOW?

- After creating the top-level overall customer service action plan, you may consider developing action plans for each individual.

- How will you periodically review overall and individual performance? What will you do if you're not meeting your goals?

Examples of overall and individual action plans are provided on the next few pages.

OVERALL CUSTOMER SERVICE ACTION PLAN *Updated:*

Metric	Goal	Current

Metric	Goal	Current

Metric	Goal	Current

ACTION TO BE TAKEN
(who? when? metric expected to impact? status?)

1.

2.

3.

4.

5.

OVERALL CUSTOMER SERVICE ACTION PLAN

Updated: 4/28

Metric	Goal	Current
Survey score	95	90

Metric	Goal	Current
Customer retention	97%	88%

Metric	Goal	Current
Referrals	0.15	0.10

ACTION TO BE TAKEN
(who? when? metric expected to impact? status?)

1. Customer retention – personal thank-you to each client
   (Smith – 6/1 – letters written and ready to send)

2. Referrals – reward program *(Johnson – complete)*

3. Survey score – investigate root cause of low scores
   *(Chen – 7/15 – management meeting on 6/30 to discuss
   countermeasures put in place)*

4.

5.

In Exercise #2, you took the time to define metrics. This table is a perfect example of why this is necessary. What does a goal of 0.15 referrals mean? Is that 0.15 referrals per customer? Per team member?

INDIVIDUAL CUSTOMER SERVICE ACTION PLAN *Updated:*

Metric	Goal	Current

Metric	Goal	Current

Metric	Goal	Current

ACTION TO BE TAKEN
(who? when? metric expected to impact? status?)

1.

2.

3.

4.

5.

Individual metrics might not be the same as overall metrics. They may cascade down from overall metrics. Individual metrics and actions should be within the team member's control.

INDIVIDUAL CUSTOMER SERVICE ACTION PLAN   *Updated: 7/1*

Metric	Goal	Current
Product test	90%	90%

Metric	Goal	Current
Smile index	1X/transaction	1X/transaction

Metric	Goal	Current
Referrals	1X/day	0X/day

ACTION TO BE TAKEN
(who? when? metric expected to impact? status?)

1. Survey score → product test – complete 3 product line tests per quarter *(6/30 – 2 complete and can answer more customer questions)*

2. Survey score → smile index – smile at least once during each transaction *(5/20 – always smiling during audits of process)*

3. Referrals – ask at least one customer per day for a referral *(6/1 – still a little shy to ask)*

4.

5.

EXERCISE #13

In addition to, or as an alternative to individual action plans, a team may consider using a "Commitment To WOW Contract." The version shown on the next page can be discussed with team members, distributed, signed, and periodically reviewed either informally or formally.

As with any tool that may be used, the point is to make wowing the customer a part of your culture.

COMMITMENT TO WOW CONTRACT

I, _____, commit to wow our customers. I realize that this isn't possible in every customer service interaction. Wow moments come from a subset of our good customer interactions. I also realize that I can just as easily ruin the reputation we work so hard to build with just a single anti-wow experience.

I will think about the concept of wow _____ times per week.

I will strive to wow a customer _____ times per week.

I will pass along ideas that could help wow customers. Likewise, I will pass along issues that have resulted in anti-wow or near miss anti-wow moments so our team can try to do our best.

Signature: _____

Date: _____

EXERCISE #14

Next, we need to develop a plan and mechanisms for information flow. Template examples are shown on the next few pages.

How will you talk about the concept of wow daily, weekly, or monthly to make it part of your culture?

What templates, tools, and equipment do you need to develop or maintain to stay on top of customer service experiences?

How will you capture lessons learned and feed them back to the team?

COMMUNICATION PLAN

Communication Mechanism	Frequency	Where	Who	Desired Outcome	Comments
Morning Meeting	Daily	Each Department	Supervisors	Reinforce importance of wowing customers	Rotate between product, process, and people messages
Staff Meeting	Weekly	Conference Room	Cano	Reinforce importance of wowing customers	Review lessons learned documents and action plans
Financial Review	Monthly	Board Room	Salgado	Senior mgt. understanding of outstanding service and where we are falling short	30,000 foot view
Testimonials	As applicable	Periodic Events	Murray	Collect and post more testimonials of great service for customer, supplier and team member viewing	Always have camera, video camera, and testimonial forms available at events

TESTIMONIAL MATRIX

- Identify the factors that are important in a potential customer's decision to buy from you.

- Identify your products and services.

- Populate the table to see where you need additional testimonials.

Factors Important To Us	Products And Services →	Liaison And Sort	Six Sigma And Lean	Employee Development
	Provide Value/ Provide Cost Savings	Customer A 8/10	Customer D 4/10	Need Testimonial
	Tremendous Knowledge Transfer	Customer C 2/12	Customer B 6/03	Customer E 10/11
	On-Time Delivery	Customer A 3/11	Need Testimonial	Not Applicable

TESTIMONIAL FORM

Name:

Company / Organization:

Please share a positive experience you've had with us regarding any or all of the following:

- On-time delivery

- Tremendous knowledge transfer

- Provide value / provide cost savings

Or please feel free to share another experience with us:

Signing and dating this form means that you approve of us sharing your comment and/or using your picture (applicable if attending one of our events).

Signature: _____   Date: _____

Issue:	Customer provided poor survey score – note in comment section says his family will not return to the restaurant.	
Why?	Customer offended by waiter's language and actions toward supervisor in front of customer's young children.	
Why?	Waiter does not understand corporate culture and was rushed into work without proper new team member training.	
Why?	Location has had a lack of leadership and newly promoted and transferred supervisor has not been able to address all issues yet.	
Lesson:	**Do not rush team members into customer interactions without proper training.**	
Counter-measure:	Team member received disciplinary action. GM to conduct all-employee meeting at this location to reinforce policies and procedures. Additional supervisor to be temporarily assigned to location to help address disciplinary issues and to develop newly promoted supervisor. Training matrix to be developed and all needed training to be performed.	

Created by: Shannon Decker 1/14/10

This form and drawings should be hand-written for ease of completion. It should provide a simple, teachable explanation of how a single issue has been handled to reduce the likelihood of future occurrences.

EXERCISE #15

The "Year of WOW" Debrief

If you've read to this point and put in the effort over the course of the year to complete the exercises, you've reached a time for reflection. Twelve months ago, you embarked on a journey. Let's take one final review of the year to see how far you've come.

Metric	Baseline	End Of Year Result	Goal	Performance

What should we be proud of accomplishing this year?

Where do we need to continue to improve?

Other observations:

If you're attaining the results you set out to achieve, congratulations! Take the time to celebrate and communicate your achievements.

If you're not getting the results you intended, take a step back and ask a few questions. Is the process working? Do you need to tweak the process or continue the way it is? You should still celebrate the positives while working to countermeasure the negatives.

Now, do one last thing.

Take a deep breath and…

Keep going. Like Allen and Jeff learned in our story, you can never rest on your customer service laurels. It's a never ending process. Good luck!

WOW
MOMENTS

Have your own
thank-you or curse you'd
like to share with us?

We'd love to
hear from you!

Email us at cs@pythonefk.com
with subject line "50/10"

THANK YOU